wass coming to me...

by: Draden Branch

First
and
foremost

I'd like to

Thank God,

for giving me

creation........

ISBN 978-0-615-20495-6

LCCN

Printed in the United States of America.

Table of contents:

Characters

Cut

Kay

Capone

Bone

Lemm

Waiter

Uncle Boomie

Manager

Detective Wells

Detective Vargas

Daq

Poot

Preface

This story takes place in a city anywhere in America. This is a story about the struggle it takes for a young African-American to retain himself and survive in this land we call America. It is said that one must ascertain the ability to be black and white. Black to know where he has come from and white to know where he is going.. I wanted to shed light on the fact that both points are true and equally important for survival. Daq the main character has decisions to make concerning his future. His mind is on straight he's happy living with his new wife Kay and they have been blessed with a son Capone. Daq used to get into a lot of trouble in his earlier years but in the last five years he's settled down and met Kay. She gave him a reason to want to try and the gift of wanting to be a better person. Also she got him a job at her fathers store in the neighborhood. Through the years you could see a genuine change in Daq. His job is working out at the corner store and life is moving in the direction he wants. Even so they arte not progressing fast as he would like so his mind wonders from time to time trying to come up with new ideas to get ahead.

Chapter 1 – Catching up

Separating zero's and commas , Wednesday, March 08, 2006

*E*very since I can remember I always wanted to make money. Growing up I didn't really know what making money meant but I knew that I wanted to do it. Watching all the people that frequented my house as a kid gave me an idea that making money had to do something with a lot of people. Later I found out my family was into some extra curricular shit. By the way my name is **Daq** (nasdaq) this here is my story unexaggerated

making myself seem larger than who I am but more reality based so you can get the uncut. My only hope is that you can benefit from my mistakes and shortcomings gaining all I have without losing all I did to get it. This life I live I do the best I can in making it happen. That is why you find me getting into a bunch of shit that really don't concern me but it ends up being lucrative most of the time although some times I get the short end of the stick. I ain't the type for cat to be out here trying impress nobody so it's funny how a man will let what others say effect him intrinsically. I do my best to not allow others too much space in my head that is why I avoid negative people and situations to the best of my ability. If you can recall I did say that I have a tendency to get involved I stupid shit to make a fast buck and that is my downfall. Getting back to those that allow others to get into their head and disrupt the flow we all develop as our style of living the shit that makes us us dig? I limit contact with acquaintances of my past being it is not good to cross game and a lot of associates of my past are not on my hype today so we say few words and part ways respectfully but occasionally there is that one who wants to relive the old days. I grew up and out physically and mentally so it baffles me to come across one of these back to the future Kats trapped in the yesteryears.

- "Nasdaq, is that you pimp'n?"

"Woow, it's been what 15 years right?"

- "Sumpting like dat. I can't call it"

See I ain't seen dis playa Poot in about fifteen years but dat was about the only thang out this nga mouth I could trust. We called the nga poot cause he was always selling wolf-tickets about harmless shit though like bitches he cut, licks he hit, or shit he had. So he got label poot, like sucka butt or rooty-poot. While we was catching up Poot was going on about how

"life was hard and drastic times call for drastic measures."

I could tell he was hinting up on something but he was beating around the bush and working his way up to it. He knew me from back in the day and knew I'm about bidness licking was some shit that came natural. It didn't take long for him to bring up the subject after the how hard life was spill.

"America, shit I though we was supossed to be free?" .

"don't nutting come free pimp, you ain't heard?"

"If you think anything is "Free" you must be "dumb""

"how long you been at this mtfka?"

"A minute mayne, it do what it do dig? A means to a end"

"So what dey paying you up in this bitch?"

"It ain't nuttin like before though, right?"

"no, but then my priorities changed and what I value has shifted"

"I ain't mad at you playboi, get it how you live dig?"

"I'm saying I got a lil sumptin sumptin

"I'm working on and I could use your assistance in-turn you'd be dooly compensated."

"and, before you even say no, I got it all

mapped out all you gadda do is drive

pimp."

(**Daq** falls off into a daydream like state **Poot** goes on about how.)

"We need to get wass coming to us our forty-acres and a mule."

I've heard that money is at the root of evil and that has to be the most concrete shit I have ever build my foundation of thinking on. The circumstances surrounding the event can be a motivating factor in the out come of any situation and my situation was not going to change until I changed it. I had been pushing this lil convenience store gig for about a year now since Capone was born. My son is what got me out the game and changed my life. I was like this lil mtfka depends on me, so how I'm going to be here if I'm out in the streets doing some undependable shit? I ain't half-ass raising no kid of mine from a jail cell. This world is hard enough I'll be damb if one of mine gone battle it on his/her own.

"So you still got the same number?"

"Naw, mayne you know how it is you go to jail get locked up and you shit get cut off, whoopty whoop yadda yadda, da extra shit."

"I can dig it, well shoot me da other one and I'm a holla after work tonight about 10 o'clock, cool?"

"Solid"

Poot got caught up ten or so months ago fkn round tryna hang with these dudes ain't nobody ever heard of.? Then all of a sudden he gangbanging and then he caught a gun case riding around with his homies. One of the **_Big Homies_** gave him the pistol to avoid getting his third strike. Poot really was a cool brother deep inside but life has delt him a bad hand at a young age and like most of us it started deteriorating what lil moral consciousness that was left after the senseless pillage of his manhood by the parasites of a decaying underground society. In other words he has been getting punked since he was a kid and now he is out fkn the world. He wasn't the sharpest tool in the shed so life took advantage of him severely every turn of the game. For some reason he hasn't giving up and he could swear his luck was about to change. I was due to hook up with this kat after work to yuck it up and get da details on da bidness. I wasn't even sure if I was going to fk with this kat like that or not did the means out weigh the risk?

Later on that day the homie **Cut** stopped through the store to get a brew and a few blunts.

"Ey you hear Poot got out"

"Yea he was in here earlier"

"My stupid ass sister was writing dat brotha while he was locked up and now he think he got a place to live. "He don't know that bitch is on her way out"

"Wow!"

"Like dat pimp'n?"

"Look if I gadda get up everyday and hit Da grind so do the next nga thinking he gone lay up in my crib."

"A true gadda respect it or get on, dig!"

"Das da bidness"

"Shit it cost to live everyday and it ain't getting no cheaper"

"That's gone be $5.50"

"Damb for a forty and a two blunts, now you see what I mean shit cost!"

"The price of living keep rising inflation taking over, and I pray Obama get in there and fix some shit."

"Obama, shit he be lucky if they don't kill his ass when they announce his victory."

"Ain't that the truth"

"Ain't no place for a Blackman in White man's politics."

As true as that may seem I think it is time for us as Black men to make a political contribution to this country since we have clearly done our share of unpaid labor."

"well I'm a do it moving mayne you stay up now."

" you do da same family, one."

All through the night I kept looking at the clock and time seemed to be dragging out. I was thinking about what Poot had said earlier and what Cut was talking bout now and Cut wasn't talking bout no money. As much as what da fk Poot was yapping don't make no matter this time around the block he was speaking my language talking dollars and making a lil cents. I figured it didn't hurt to go see what this mtfka had in mind it might turn out to be to my advantage. First I'm a go get me a sac from da whiteboi and get up with Poot after that. I finished up my shift closed the store and began my walk home. (talking out loud to myself) I just got one restitution payment left to the department of revenue and I can start stacking for my ride. Luckily I got off wit house arrest and fines the judge said next time he see my face he going to put me under the jail with a football number. I noticed as I was coming out the store there was a strange figure across the street in between two buildings off in the shadows but I paid it no mind and went on my way.

"ey", "ey", "wassup bra bra?"

"You forget about you boy? You was supposed to be coming to my spot after work"

"You going towards da East I live downtown"

Ow wassup pimp'n!"

"I'm going to get some trees and then I was headed yo way"

"Right, Right, well I was coming to get yo ass cause I though you was bullshitting bout falling through, so I'm a strike with you."

"Das da bidness, come on"

"My dude stay over there by community center"

"There is a creek over there too and a park, right?"

"Yea that's the one"

"You know it's been a minute since I been out so I 'm tryna refamiliarize myself wit thangs and places"

"How long you been out?"

"A couple weeks, and I still ain't use to shit"

I kept thinking about the last time I seen this kat and the difference in his mannerism. I could tell that he had a lot on his mind and that he was older in thought. Not just more mature but a lil wiser. Still the same in a lot of ways but there was a noticeable change in his poise and how he carries himself. This kat use to always be stuntastic in his recollections and a entertaining story teller and he didn't have nothing to say unless I asked him a question it was kinda early.

"Cut was in the store earlier"

"For real what dat nga talking bout now?"

"aww nutting he was just saying he seen you and did I know you was out?"

"He has zero tolerance for a nga fresh out"

"Ain't like da nga feed me I just kick it at the crib every now and then"

"Truth be told I'm tired of running the streets and I be tryna stay outta shit post, but he think I'm laying around lollygaggin so he be on me like gangbusters"

"If he knew his sister was pregnant I think he'd come unglued!"

"I ain't been out a month and she's three weeks hot"

"Damb!, I mean congratulations you know?"

"Goodlookin out family, I been praying"

- "You and Tracy got any names picked out?

"Not really for the girl but you know I'm getting me a junior if it's a boy!'

"Hold on real quick I need to hit dis cat one mo gin"

When they stopped walking they were on the side of the community center by the parking-lot. Daq asked Poot to post up for a minute so he could hit the white-boi. Daq took his phone out his pocket made the call. Around two minutes later a white-boi blowing a chop came around the corner walking a pit bull.

— "Wassup with you Mr. Nasdaq?"

"Tryna get my head in the right place"

"Well my man you called the right dude"

"I got dat fire!, I hope you ready to take off?"

"Das luv you always give me what I pay for, $40 for the eight right?"

"That's yo player price always"

"Goodlookin out"

"ey dis my dude Poot he just got out he might cop from you later on, cool?,"

"Fo show holla when you need dat"

"Yall be easy now."

Daq and Poot both dapped the whiteboi and parted ways in different directions.

Chapter 2 - Goin fo mines

who else gone do it

"let's go get a swish."

"I'm wit it that give me time to holla at you about that work"

" I feel like I gadda make a move soon being time is ticking on the clock this baby is going to be her soon."

"Truth of the matter is I want this baby and I'm feeling Tracy she a do good type I know you feel me?"

"She was in my corner almost the whole dime, it's like she did the time with me"

"I owe it to her to make something happen"

"The way Cut be coming ain't right sometime but I feel where he coming from I really don't deserve somebody as sweet as Tracy fo all the wrong I've done."

"I be feeling like he ain't GOD so don't judge me nga!"

"But I'm all up in his shit so, when you in Rome you gadda live like the Romans"

"I know I gadda make a move soon though and that is what brings me to you."

"Damb that is a gang of heavy shit you just laid on me homie."

"I really don't know how to respond."

"Say you will help"

"I don't see how but if I can then wassup, holla at yo boi."

"Like I said before all I need you to do is drive and I'll do the rest."

"I got you the load you got a license, right?"

"Yea I got L'z"

"Okay then you can drive Tracy's car here go the extra keys."

"Tomorrow after you get off work you can pick me up and we can scope out the lick and I'll fill you in on the details."

"I can dig it but what you talking as far as compensation folks?"

" I knew you'd come around how about

$500 for fifteen minutes of work?"

"That sounds real nice to me.'

"Really then a rack would be music so sing a song, you get a rack."

By the end of the sack we set the plan and it was in motion. I'm gonna drive Tracy's car home tonight and to work tomorrow and then scoop up Poot. Then we are going to scope the lick and I'll get the details.

"Okay it's that silver car right there."

"I'm going to sleep I'll holla miyanna"

"One!"

"That will work."

On the way home I fell into deep though about past, present and future shit. All I gadda do is drive for fifteen minutes and I'll get a rack. It would take me almost three paychecks to get that money and the unexpected cash will put me ahead of the game. I been really tryna do right since the last time I got caught up. It's hard being a civilian going to work paying taxes and still not getting **wass coming to me**. Poot is a real nga and I know he gone get his loot so when

I do my part I'm getting paid too. On the way home Poot didn't say much but I attributed that to the fact he was plotting his next move. I felt better about the silence this

time since he let me in on what was bothering him. I know when my girl Kay got pregnant with my lil soldier Capone I was nervous as hell and she was reading books and shit to prepare, so when he came I was game-goofy and she kinda knew what to expect. Now I'm a provider with a family and that is some real shit. They are my reason for doing what I do everyday. Looked up and before I knew it I was bending the corner of my block. I parked the car down the street from our apartment cause I didn't want to alarm Kay. She is a very intelligent lady and not very easily fooled; one of the reasons I love her so much it shows me she cares. The more I

keep out her face less I have to answer for. She knew Poot from back in the day and that is the last nga she'd wanna see me fkn around with. Normally I wouldn't be fkn

with this kat but he got at me at a weak moment and some of the shit he said made sense it ain't like I got anther place to make a $1000 in fifteen minutes. Plus I'm tired of seeing Kay and Capone walk in the mornings to school and work. It felt good driving and that just made me want it more. I got into the house about 11:30 and Kay was putting Capone to bed. I gave her a kiss hello and told her she could get some rest daddy was home. I went into the room to read Capone a story before bed.

"wassup lil man?"

"Daddy!"

"May I ask why you ain't asleep yet?"

"Mommy said I could stay up until you got home."

"She did?"

"unn huuh!" (knodding his head up and down like a lil bobble-head doll)

"Well that's cool I wanted to say goodnight to you anyway and I still owe you a story."

"Allright!!, your the best dad in the world."

"I don't know about that but I do love you Capone."

'I love you too daddy"

"Well you climb into bed and I'll get the storybook"

"Okay Daddy'

I read Capone a story about <u>*Dr. Martin Luther King Jr.*</u> and how his murder was an assassination of a Civil Rights leader and what a loss we suffer today as a result of it. I want him to understand the struggle that we as a people have endured but also the struggle still to come. I then tucked him into bed, Good night. I enjoy being a father I view it as a privilege from the Lord above so I take my role in Capone's life very serious. I try to feed his mind, body, and soul. I want him to recognize every option available instead of feeling what I felt growing up . . . underprivileged. After I finished with my son I went into the other room where Kay was.

"Wassup baby?"

"Just getting Capone's and my stuff ready for the morning the more I do now the less I have to do tomorrow morning."

"That's my boo always one step ahead of the game"

"I try to be"

"let me tell you momma you doing way more then trying around here!"

"That is why I'm working on something for us and it's gone make improve our lifestyle."

"There ain't nothing wrong with the way we are living."

"All I'm saying is we could use a couple thangs up in here to make life a lil easier for us."

"We do well on the necessities but we don't get to enjoy common shit that everybody else seem to enjoy."

"I need to get wass coming to me!... us ..i mean for us.

"I don't know who everybody is but I do know it is wrong by God to look at the next man and envy what they have."

"We have a good life and it's getting better everyday so we need to be thankful for that"

"True but I also feel like If I don't help myself and if I don't then nobody will."

"I mean Poot is right about dat much."

"POOT!!"

"You mean Poot that went to da pen Poot!"

"Poot that couldn't stand up for his own God Damb Self Poot"

"I know you a lot smarter than that baby"

"Poot don't give a fk about you, me, Capone, Cut, Tracy, or they mtfkn baby, Lord excuse my mouth please, Amen."

"See you got me cursing up in this piece."

"That's where all this bs about getting wass coming to you and wanting more than you are thankful for?"

"This shit is getting all mixed up look baby bottom-line I love you and I love this life we have but..."

(Kay interjects as Daq was speaking)

"See there that's where you stop making sense, if you loved this life and this family there would be no buts."

"Not to blatantly be rude and not acknowledge you were speaking cause I do but pardon me."

"I see you got your mind made up and you probably already got some shit going, but I want you to know that you are doing cause you are not happy with what we have."

"I'm fine with carrying out my daily activities he way I have always been until we can find a better way."

"Then to risk not being able to sleep next to you at night or share my day with regularly.

"the bottom-line Daq is you have to make a choice or it will eventually be made for you."

"Goodnight *Nasdaq Xaiver Taylor.*"

I always hated to end the night like this with us on opposite sides of the opinion. We always make decisions together and it seemed like we never can agree when it comes to means that justify the ends. I'm more like let's get the shit right now and she can wait with patients. I think that is one of the things that makes us such a good team she complements my weak points and I vise versa. Tonight I had to say though things were leaning in her favor and she was coming from a of place of love. I mean really what was I thinking getting involved in one of this cats schemes being I ain't seen nor heard from him in so long? I said to myself that I don't trust his judgment but I'm at a crossroad in my life between circumstances and my situation. I need to stick to what has been working because it ain't like I ain't traveled that road to fast cash before, been there done that bought the t-shirt and came back. I had a lot on my mind when I went to sleep. Kay went to bed and I slept on the couch that night alone with her words and my thoughts.

"Poot don't give a fk about you, me, Capone,

Cut, Tracy, or they mtfkn baby" and how she said
"There

ain't nothing wrong with the way we are living."
But what

really kept going through my head was

"bottom-line Daq is you have to make a choice
or it will eventually be made for you."

"or it will eventually be made for you."

"eventually be made for you."

"eventually be made for you."

I made my mind up I'm going to tell Poot I ain't fkn with him I got too much to lose and he can find another driver. I fell asleep on that thought. When I woke up it was already thirty minutes passed the time I expected to get up and Kay and Capone had already left.

I found a note that read….

Sorry we fought,

But you know that means make-up

sex!!!!! I'll see you after work and

we can talk together and find a

solution.

I Love you Daq..
For eva yours

Kay.

I Couldn't wait to get home tonight to see my lady and my son. It always made me feel good when my girl and I came to an understanding it just assured me time and time again what a blessing my good woman was. It was final in my mind that I needed to be thankful and count the blessings I did have instead of counting all the unnecessary things I didn't need.

Chapter 3 - Understanding

Slowly but surely

I awoke feeling like a new man and I knew that it was going to be difficult breaking the news to Poot that I could no longer be involved wit his scheme, which was a good thing because I was able to let him know before I got in too deep and here was no turning back. I know he's serious about getting that money all the pressure he got coming from Cut. I got up and immediately notice that Kay and Capone were gone. I washed my face, got a pop tart and a cup of orange juice out of the refrigerator. It was 7:15 am I was to start work at 8 am. Mr. Meeleib the store owner always wanted us the employee's to be there at least five minutes before the shift started so that we were not milking the clock for overtime we were not doing shit. Even though he was strict about the timing he would allow you to come in on you off days and work under the able for cash in between paydays. I clocked-out and left, walked down the street hopped in Poot's female's (Tracy) load scooted to my gig. I arrived fifteen minutes early and sat in the car retracing the events as they occurred. I began to pray out loud to myself and thank the lord for what I had. I went to work feeling good so good I got three complements and that made Mr. Meeleib happy because happy customers come back. Got of at ten o'clock and started

out the door as I was walking out I noticed Poot was waiting by his chicks load (Tracy's car) smoking a Beedie.

I'm like damb that's a throwback!"

"What you talking bout?"

" da beedie"

"I ain't smelled that since we was in the 7th grade that lil mom and pop's spot around the corner used to sell the before they closed down."

"Is that right?"

"Yea but that was a longtime ago"

"I wanted to holla at you about that lil job you needed me to do"

"How bout we get a sack on me and chop it up on that cool?"

"That sounds cool with me are you sure you got it?"

"What you think I can't cop a lil fonky ass twamp nga? Damb!"

"Naw my nigg I'm bullshitting"

"You think you dude Bone ell come threw if you hit him?"

"I'm sure he want dat money"

"Bet"

I hit Bone like Poot asked me to and he said he'd meet us in the same place as last time. So we skirted out to get there before he did cause poot said "it was bad bidness" for him to have to wait for us. When was on the side of he community center we had time to kill so we freestyling back and forth about our days and who was the hottest MC. Bone rolled up on a bicycle looking like a hip-hop cholo. I'm mean he bike was hot product but fk he didn't fit the description of the kat who should be mobbing the bike period.

"Wassup with you fellas tonight?"

"Nutting too much getting at you for the nightcap!"

"So you wanted the dubber right?"

"Yea that's what you wanted Poot?"

"Is it too late to get a lil mo?"

"or is that all you brang?"

"No I got what mo (*my nigg*) what you need?"

"everything that's coming to me my nigg!"

Poot must have lost his mtfkn mind because he pulled out some heat and went berserk!!! He slapped Bone so hard with that gun I could hear the echo like the pistol went off and he would not stop hitting him either. He lost his faculties and flashed in a fit of a rage and beat that mtfkas head off. (It made me step back like uggghh!!) My first instinct was to help Bone but I'm not going to willing put myself in jeopardy to save a mtfka I barley know in hopes this other mtfkn nut don't kill me too. After Poot came to he ran through Bones pockets and began to strip him of all his valuables. Looking at me like are you going to tell on me but never bringing it to words. I knew what was on his mind because he kept justifying it by saying that whiteboi ain't never had to work for what he got and that it was fkd up we were born in a fkd up position and someone had to pay and he was getting **wass coming to me**. I honestly don't recall word for word what he was ranting what is clear in my head to this day is those few brief moments still echo in my present decisions. Tonight was supposed to be my last night kicking it like this with this kat and now I'm in some shit an accessory to a murder fk! This mtfka not only set da whiteboi up but he set me up too by using my to get to Bone. I had to worry about my girl Kay and my son Capone now I can't let this fkn nut know what they mean to me that will be the first thang he goes after when it all goes down. Poot must have been plotting this shit for a long ass time but it couldn't have been too long cause I just introduced him to Bone not that long ago. This shit is fkn with my brain and look at this nga I should have never got involved with this mtfka he really don't give a fk. Now I'm caught da fk up and I need to really get word to my chick to let her know the dillions on this kat. All this shit flashed through my mind in what seemed like an eternity but was almost instantaneous because poot was still ranting and raving.

"who's the nga now mtfka!"

"Get up!"

"Iiiiiiiii Caaaaan"t hhhhheeaaar youuu!"

"Poot what da fk mayne!"

"Is you stupid?"

"How you just gone trans up on me like this and buss dis mtfka shit like dat without putting me up on da shit?"

"Why you give a fk about this mtfka?"

"Huh?"

"Do you believe if this was **YOU** laying there on the floor he'd give a fk if one of his redneck good ole boys was whooping on yo ass!?"

"That's the GAME and we in it!"

"Too many suckas is playing and don't know the rules they act as though they don't apply to them"

"Like they are above the GAME and not subject to all it has to offer'

"That is where I come in."

"A breathe of fresh air."

"Innovator of ingenuity"

"Plus there is a balance to be kept"

"You out yo monkey-ass mind."

"What da fk dey do to you In jail bra bra?"

"Innovator?"

"fresh air?"

"balance?"

"Dude you on some way other far out ass third rock from the sun type shit."

"That's yo bad."

"I thought you was tryna get it?"

"If there is one thing I learned in studying the art of my predecessors failures is that murder is the one thing that separates the zero's and commas.

<u>"Everything I do is calculated"</u>

"I can not afford to lose and I ain't going back to the pen."

"There is too much at stake and I'm getting to old for this shit. I consider it my duty by obligation to iron out the wrinkles."

"We are misunderstood so often because of the fool we let represent us."

"We need to do our best to eliminate those perpetrating a fraud."

"There are gangsters in every race, creed, and religion. If we all did our part in weeding out the suckas the world would be a better place."

"The government is one the biggest, strongest, and we organized gangs there are."

"Like the police."

 "Think about how they don't let any and everyone in, they got the best weapons, communications, and transportation."

 "Ironically they operate outside of the laws they are sworn to uphold and protect."

Chapter 4 – Surviving

Slavery...

I started to realize the difference in the Poot now from the Poot before and this Poot was arrogant and self-righteous. I could see in his face and hear in his voice he was unbroken and far from humble. Bitter from the way he felt life had it out for him. It has been fifteen years and I heard prison is a fkd up place to be not cause of the Confinement but the polotix behind the dynamics. Blacks and Whites constantly at each others throats fighting for control in a unpredictable situation. The Latino's, Philippino's and all the other O's the can give a number and confine them like animals in the name of rehabilitation. It's modernized slavery. Slavery was a very lucrative market for those fortunate enough to be the slaver, proprietor, or merchant in charge of receiving the profit from the transaction but what about the slave? The merchandise so to speak how well was it maintained before the transaction was completed metaphorically speaking? Poot was like a angry slave screaming "Give us free!"

*There is what is known between African Americans as what is referred to as **"Black people"** and **"Niggas."** The distinction between the two is clear once you have been enlightened to its virtue. Black people strive for excellence in every*

motion we understand that there is a responsibility that comes with being black and we view it as a positive instead of the stereotypical negativity that has been so biased placed upon us.

(We feel as thou we have been put in a fkd up position that was supposed to kill us but by the grace of God we came up only to be blamed and talked bad about for how we did it.)

That is where the "niggas" come in those are the African Americans that do not want to conform to societies norms but then society has never taken responsibility for its part in slavery either. (but that is a different novel). They feel as though we were not given a equal opportunity from the gate, (the beginning) we entered this country as second class citizens and so this country has come accustomed to allowing us second class citizenship. Second class education, healthcare, jobs, living environments and wages for pay all second class. Newton's third law of motion

"For every action there is an equal

and opposite reaction."

http://csep10.phys.utk.edu/astr161/lect/history/newton3laws.html

according to a web site found on Google.Poot was definitely a nigga and he didn't give fk about anything but getting wass coming to him. By this time I had already made my way to Tracy's car and I was hollering at this dumbass nga to hurry for we was made by some mtfkn body I was nervous as fk driving running red-lights and impatient at stop signs.

"slow yo ass down for you get us blerpped!"

"I should have never fkd with yo ass."

"Couln't have, wouldn't have you show shouldn't have."

"If anything I shouldn't fkd wih you ."

"I was gone give you yo share but you unappreciative mtfka I did all the work, all you didwas drive."

"Wait"

"what you mean?"

"I though we was gone scope the lick and discuss the details before we made a move you know I don't get down like this!"

"I knew if I told you the get down you would pussy out so I did what I had to do."

"This is bullshit!"

"I trusted you and you fkd me"

"not really it's all a mater of prospective."

"You wanted to come up I just gave you the opportunity and you bit."

"Ain't that about a bitch, you got me fkd up"

"Look I got $470 and two and a half ounces off the whiteboi once we lick the store I'll be able to give you that rack and you can be on your way."

" you get a ounce and $200 right now and the rest after he lick."

"Your out yo fkn mind dude you really fkn lost it"

"I'm sick of mtfkas saying I'm crazy, or I lost it, and dumb ass shit like that."

"I'm separating the zeros from the commas and if you ain't wit it you extra baggage; I can't afford no lose ends."

"Okay fk this shit if you want me to go along with this shit then you gadda start coming clean with me!"

"okay I think I can trust you enough now shoot but you gadda figure shit out on your own I'll answer any question asked right."

"when did you decide to lick my job?"

"six months ago when I got out."

"six months!"

"I thought you only been out a month?"

"I needed you to think that or you would have been suspicious."

"so you been watching the store six months?"

" no only three."

"why you merk Bone?'

"truth be told I lost it when he called me a nga I had a pententry flashback them nazi's that run the prisons fkd my head up."

"what about your baby and Tracy?"

"there ain't no baby that was a lie to play on your emotions I knew you was sentimental like that."

"Tracy never was pregnant we spread that so Cut would let me come around cause he was hating so tuff we figured if I was family he'd eventually come around."

"damb so you got Tracy lying for you too!"

"I told you the whole way everything I do is calculated."

"well what if I didn't want to go along with this shit then what how was you gone get me involved then?"

"I came tonight to tell you I was straight and to give you Tracy's car back, and call the whole thing off."

"haa haa that's funny ."

"you say what if you didn't want to go along with it and you was going to give me Tracy's car back, right?"

"yea so what?"

"I bet you didn't even let Kay know youdriving this car did you?"

"No why and how you know?"

"cause she would have let you know this ain't Tracy's car it's Hot!

"what da fk?"

"yeah homeboi you been rolling in a g-ride"

”see when we first talked to you let me know what you were slaving that gig at the corner store for, a whip.”

“that let me know how to get at you and what to bait you with”

“every since you put the keys in the ignition and started this car you have been involved.”

“before that you were being plotted on.”

“why me?”

“I didn't pick you I chose you.”

"do you understand the difference?"

"That was a rhetorical question in case you were about to answer."

"I was in court the day you got probation you don't remember because I was incarcerated and forbidden to conversant with the public from where I was seated in the section beside the judge."

"you told the judge that you were a lookout and that was the extent of your involvement but not only were you the one who kicked the door in but you set the lick up."

"It was your heat."

"you owe the GAME"

"who are you to judge me Phillip?"

"isn't that the pot calling the kettle black?"

"do you remember earlier when I said some people act like the rules don't apply to them like they are above the game?"

"I meant mtfks like you that have seen the fruits of the GAME but never suffered the pain."

"I recall slightly so the fk what, what you saying?"

"I ain't nutting like you and never claimed to be!"

"you say I set the shit up but if you knew what da fk you talking bout you would know mtfks pay me for what I know I don't make ngs do shit."

"I kicked the door are you stupid?"

"I don't know who you got you facts from but you burned!, ha haa!"

"I get down like dat homie check my pedigree and run my credentials."

"I'm clean because I don't let other mtfks decide what and when I'm gone handle my bidness."

"like right now you all in my cool-aid and don't know da flavor."

"Then you get me caught up in this bullshit."

"Misery love company"

Chapter 5 —Reestablishing

I been out the GAME a long time and the shit that

Poot was saying was hitting me hard because it ain't

like this nga was there so he had to be have talking to

somebody that was there when I was pulling my licks

and shit. Truth was on this instant he did not know

what the fk he was talking about. It started brewing in

my head all the shit he was saying and how he got me

caught the fk up by killing Bone. This mtfka been

plotting on me for a long time now but I still don't

know what da fk his problem really is though cause

that shit he was talking don't add da fk up. Even if that

was the case why he give a fk it didn't concern him. I

gadda find out what he's thinking to know my next

move. This whole time we are driving I was looking

for a spot to dock out. This cat is covered in blood and I can't keep a thought straight in my head. Anybody I take this fool around is a potential target. I been telling Poot my secrets, my fears shit about Kay and I the whole time he was pumping me for information. It is times like this when the words of moms ring in my head **"You can't trust nobody baby this is a cruel world."** All I was tryna do was get ahead of the GAME and now I'm a victim of circumstances. Poot was right about one thing and it is a matter of perspective. I needed to get a message to Kay about this nut and not let him know. I fkd up by getting involved with this cat but it's too late for that from here on out we play GAME my way. I figured out Poot needed me to pull the lick on the store so that is why I'm still alive and after that he'd no longer have a use for me. He was looking at me all fkd up and then said,

"let's go to yo crib."

"naw let's not!"

"nga I ain't suggesting it I'm telling you take me to you crib."

"you see all this fkn blood?"

"I need to get out these clothes and burn them."

"okay bet"

"I kinda lost it for a minute but I'm back on track."

"I hope you still got room for me in your plans?"

"How I'm spoza trust you and you flipped?"

"I'm a have to watch you for a minute but yea I could still use you for now but I got my eye on you."

"good looking out I need da scrill to support da family."

"I'm a hit Kay and tell her to leave for a minute while we handle bidness."

"dat sounds good but you don't think she's going to be trippin?"

"I got dis pimp'n don't trip."

Daq pulls his phone out of his front pocket of his Dickey shorts, cut off at the kneese hanging low.

"wassup Kay?"

"ey how you doing boo where you at I been worried?"

"my bad I didn't let you know wassup but I been caught up"

"is everything okay?"

"no I need you to give me some space."

"space?"

"yea I was thinking you kinda crowding me and I need you to go to your mothers for a while so I can breathe."

"what am I saying that you don't understand, shit I'm fkn somebody else there I said it."

"but....I....you fkn asshole and you weren't even man enough to see me face to face you piece of shit."

"I will be gone and so will Capone you son of a bitch!, bye!"

(Kay hangs up the phone)

"Damb pimp you went badon her I didn't think you had it in you and I knew you wasn't all goody goody like you was tryna be either."

"I was thinking to myself can't nobody be this fkn square after the stories I heard about you."

"After I get cleaned up we gadda go get some pussy and a drank it on me!"

"that sounds good"

The last time some shit was on this nga I became an accessory to murder I ain't looking forward to what da fk is next. There are only three people I trust enough to bring them in on what I got worked out, so the thing is going to be getting a hold of them to fill them in on my predicament. One of them is my Uncle "Boomie Ross" the Trojan hoarse. The next is Uncle Dave the handiest mtfka on the planet and last but not least my dude T- Lemm I call him Lemm for short. These are the mtfkas I would take anywhere for anything and know the job is getting handled. They balance me out when I lose it from time to time and this one of those times when I felt like I was going to lose it this mtfika is sitting here like ain't shit wrong. I hope Kay got the message and realizes soon that there is a problem. We pulled on to the street where I lived and I told Poot to sit in the car while I went to see if Kay was still there. He agreed and turned on the radio. I got out the car and started up the street got to the house and it was empty as ever and hollow with a echo to it when I called out

 "Hello"

there was no response. I shook the loneness snapped out of it and sprang into action. Called my dude Lemm but there was no response it went straight to voicemail.

 "you know who you reached leave a message at the sound of the beep and I'll get back at cha."

"Look man, dis nga Poot flipped his wig and its all bad. I had to bullshit Kay to get her out the crib pimp I need you to get a hold of my uncles so they can have the heads up, I'm counting on you one!"

Soon as I turned around Poot was standing behind me asking

"who was you talking to?"

"I was checking my message why you in my bidness?"

"I do live here"

"okay my bad kick it killer I was just asking?"

"there is towels in the cabinet by the sink in the bathroom."

"I got some sweats you can sport and a old throwback."

"you understand why I asked you right?"

"no why mtfka?"

"You turned coat on me earlier and I gadda watch you."

"I don't want to have to be on you but damb this is my freedom at stake."

"I want to trust you but my gut tells me that you are not totally convinced I'm in this to assist you."

"Some shit has to be handled diplomatically and they call dignified black me in suits like you to do all the negotiating to keep the peace."

"When that shit fails they call ngs like me to restore order and do the jobs that require a zero tolerance and a more hands on approach."

"either way you look at it like yen and yang we need each other., face it we are connected like that."

Chapter 6 – Isn't it ironic?

Karma is a bitch…

While poot was getting cleaned up it gave me time to get a plan together and to ease my mind I blew a blunt and when that didn't work I blew another by the time Poot got out the shower I had blew a eight and drank a half pint Hennessey. Needless to say I was fkd up and ready to get my swerve on at the bar. That is the impression I wanted to give Poot. It didn't take me long to convince this cat I was down wit his program. First we were going to get rid of the clothes and the car. We put the clothes in a plastic bag outside by the trash until we left and cleaned the bathroom of any trace evidence (I watch a lot of Crime SCI).On the way out I grabbed the bag locked up and we were on our way to get rid of the car and clothes. We drove to the mountains and on the way up I suggested we call someone to meet us at the bottom of the hill so we can get a ride home. Poot was wit it. I called my

Uncle Boomie and he said "no problem where you at?" I told him we were not finished what we were doing and I would hit him back in a hour or so and hung up. Got to the top of the mountain and drove the car off the cliff with the clothes in the back. It took us about forty-five minutes to tie up the lose ends with car and make it down the hill to meet our ride. Poot didn't say much it was like he didn't know what to make of the way I suddenly changed my attitude he started acting funny and being all silent. It didn't make me none because it gave me time to think and I enjoyed the silence sometimes you can learn more about a person by what they don't say rather than them answering questions because people lie all the time. Watching a persons behavior gives you more of an Idea of what they think to themselves and that is what I was interested in knowing about poot what the fk he was thinking. One thing for sure is he was worried because he was not talking as much as before he didn't have all the answers anymore no longer bold, macho, and in control now he was going off the top of his head. Maybe he didn't plan to kill Bone. Shit is falling apart from what it looks like and I'm going to take this opportunity to plant my seed. Looking at him now it almost makes me want to feel sorry for him but fk dat this mtfka is gone pay for all the shit he was talking. I have to play my cards right because this "dee deet dee dee" has gone over the edge and he's destroying everything around him. If I don't take control of this situation then it is definitely a wrap so .

"where you wanna go get dat drink and pussy?'

"it's lil spot downtown I seen it when I got off the Greyhound."

"I don't think I been there but I hope it cracking."

"I knew you'd come around that's what I'm talking bout!"

"I'll knock me a bitch in these old ass sweats and throwback."

"well I need to get that bitch Kay off my mind she smothers a brotha."

"it was cool at first but you know a playa gadda spread his wings, dig?"

"I feel you pimp'n whats taking your uncle?"

"I don't know but he coming give him a minute he kinda getting up there."

"let me hit him again."

"Cool I'm a go take me a piss my nigg I'll be back."

"unk, unk, you there ?"

UB – "yea wassup neff?"

"where you at?"

– "about 10 minutes away I had to get gas"

"right on, goodlookin out and I'll see you when you get here."

"oneluv!"

"I knew I could count on you, thank you."

As I was getting off the phone Poot was coming back from his bathroom break.

"he'll be here in 10 minutes or so he had to get gas."

 "I'll get him to drop us off at that lil spot we can get around from there."

My uncle picked us up from the bottom of the hill no questions asked and dropped us at the lil spot downtown **_Original Joe's._** I passed this spot hella times coming back and forth through downtown but I have never had the pleasure of dining here. It seems as though tonight I will. Soon as we walked in I was fascinated from the atmosphere it was like right out of one of those Godfather movies the way the joint was set up. I could swear there were Italian mob bosses at every table. Sitting there talking under there breath fat ass hell with the baddest bitch feeding them spaghetti as he try not to get any on their Armani suits. We found our way to the

back of the restaurant there was a clear table Poot told me to order what I wanted and he was going to wash his hands. I sat at the table when the waiter returned he asked

"what I wanted?"

" I said water because I had no money"

"okay thank you sir."

After twenty minutes passed Poot comes out the bathroom acting kinda funny but I paid it no mind. Poot picked up a menu and started looking at the selections that looks good ow so does this.

"what you gone get?"

"Nutting I ain't got no money"

"Nga I told you I got you."

"Bra bra your track record ain't to cool with me show me some money and I'll order."

"are you serious"

"hell yea I ain't fkn with you."

"these mtfkn Italians ain't playing dey gone fk us up tryna pull that okey doke."

"why you so scary nga I'm hungry and I'm finna eat."

"I'm getting was coming to me you better come on in."

"no thank you I'm fine with water."

"suit you self starve I'm eating"

Poot finished eating and the waiter came with the check he didn't even look at me he dropped the check in front of Poot and said "will that be all sir?" Poot said yea and the waiter left. That's when Poot look at me and said

"I'm finna dip"

"are you coming?"

The waiter must have been suspicious from the way Poot ordered all that food because he tipped the rest of the workers off and they stood by the exits as we stood up. A waitress asked if we leaving and offered to take the check to the counter and Poot tried to bolt for the door. There was an off duty police in the restaurant and he stuck his foot out and Poot leveled off his feet and landed on his face. One of the restaurant workers tackled him and held him until the officer could make the arrest. They went to snatch me up because I was with this fool at the table. Two waiters grabbed me and was escorting me to the back until the guy Marcos that was our waiter said

"No not him he ordered water."

"I told you mtfkas let me out these mtfkn hand cuffs."

The police was cool once they found out the real and it felt good to be right for once after always getting fkd with by them dirty mtfks. I was released and allowed to leave but the police took Poot for warrants and tryna eat and run. I was relieved to see that dumb-ass nga in cuffs ordinarily I would not wish that on another black man but damb this nga is a fkn problem and it just keeps getting worse. In a way it pleased me to be rid of Poot. It still bothered me about what happened to Bone and now I gadda get a hold of Kay to let her know wassup.

Chapter 7 – Perpetuating the cycle

*T*his has been a strange fkn day I'm sure it can't get

no stranger. When they let me go first thing I did was

apologize to the owner and the staff for being

associated with a no good for nothing mtfka like that

not in those exact words but to that effect. I also told

them I would return to pay what he owed and they

told me he was going to get wass coming to him. That

there was no harm done on my part at to forget

abouttit! And to

"feget about him!"

I needed to get a ride so I called my dude Lemm again this time he answered.

"wattitdoo doo bra bra?"

"wow why some old way out shit done happened to yo boi?"

" got you message and I got a hold of your uncles they know wassup but Boomie was like what I just dropped that nga off!"

"you ain't knowing I'm a break it down soon as you swoop me you can do that right?"

"fo show where you at?"

"Down town at Original Joes"

"Original Joes?"

"yea you ain't heard the half"

"I'm on it pimp'n"

hung up the phone took two steps and to my surprise
there was the same police that tripped Poot in the
restaurant getting

out of his unmarked car on his way over in my direction. I was hoping it wasn't true but yepp he's coming over here and I don't think this is a social call.

"how you doing there Mr. Nasdaq?"

"officer"

"you don't even seemed surprised that I know who you are?"

"well that is you job right?"

"I need you to come with me"

"am I under arrest?"

"I could have taken you at the restaurant if that is what I wanted"

"no offence but you are a little fish Iwant the barracudas like yo boi Poot."

"you know he's graduated in the last year we have four open murders on him and a long list of other shit but we can't get a conviction to stick."

"every time he walks or the witnesses come up missing, or even worse dead."

"in every instance they were partners of a sort and the situation goes bad."

"We have been, by we I mean Detective Wells and myself Detective Vargas."

"we have been tailing the suspect by the street name of Poot for a lil less than a year now."

"a year (puzzled)???"

- "yes a year why do you seem so surprised?"

See I was never been fond of the police in my line of work and I did not know what they wanted from Poot or me. Then they drop on me this mtfka been out a year that really got me twisted up top. That me twice in a row that I know of about the same shit. "I asked him how long he was out and how long he was out and he responded 3 months the first time and 6 the second time. They been watching him for a year so they know me and this cat just hooked up but why they let me roll the hot ride for so long and why they ain't arrested us yet? This shit is starting to get fkn deep. How I know this is a straight police? The could be like that that asshole Denzel played in **Training Day.** I need to get off this fkn corner talking to these fkn pigs for somebody get the wrong fkn impression.

"arrest me or let me go there will be no further conversation."

"I got the right to remain silent and I'm using it."

"that you are entitled to under the constitution of the United States that is you right."

"You so free to exercise that option but then you put me in a bad position."

"now I'm forced to exercise my rights as well and excuse me Detective Vargas"

"yes Detective Wells."

"Did we say we were tailing the suspect a year?"

"yes I believe we did."

"so that would mean a few nights ago around 11:30pm were tailing him then would that be a correct assumption based upon the information presented?"

"I would concur after deriving at a similar conclusion after comparing notes."

"so that would mean we were tailing said suspect the night one street name Bone was killed. Found

DOA behind the recreation center on the West side of San Jose."

 "I believe so!"

 "That being said I hope you keep quiet it will be easier to get the conviction."

Fuck! That is the last fkn thing I needed to hear about right now. I wasn't about to take a charge for a crime I didn't fkn commit but damb I ain't no snitch either. This nga Poot in my eyes deserve what ever the fk he gets himself into and I ain't gone be the one to put the nail in his coffin. I understand him and we are connected like that. I must admit at first I thought he was a selfish bitch but I had forgot what it was like to be on the other end of he stick and get the shit. I had squared up for a minute doing my daddy thang for Capone. Poot ain't got what I got and he ain't had what I had it is wrong for me to judge his actions because that is not something I would have done who says what da fk I'm doing is the right thing. There ain't no book to this shit being Black in America. Now these fkn fifties is all in my tall can and ain't put in on it dig? In other words they keep grilling me but the story ain't changed one bit.

"all that is interesting but like I said if you got something charge me if not release me"

"you never were under arrest or being detained you have been free to leave."

"I'm out"

Chapter 8 – Epiphany

A convoluted perspective

I have to put distance on the fifties and the situation

I need time to think and plus I haven't seen my baby or my lady Kay in a couple days fkn with this fool Poot. I'll get back to the house and I'll call her soon as I do. I can't wait to hear her voice and I miss my son Capone too. Once I gain perspective I'll be able to find what my next step should be and talking to Kay will give that to me. She always has intelligent input never judgmental so that gives me a side that I can't get from me being African American. Kay my girl is Hawaiian and Filipino she is the best thing to happen to me at this time in my life. I value her beyond her being a woman she is brilliant, she is kind, and she is my soul mate. That is the reason when we lost our first child we kept trying until we had Capone. They are what changed my life in a sense being that when I was o0n my own I clearly did not give on fk about where I ended up or where I was going. Through character definition as father and husband I began to define myself as a person. This time apart has given me solidity in thought. I keep jumbling different things as I'm making my way back to the house on foot because I have no car.

I was riding in a hot load and now I'm striking because it was hot at da spot and I was not about to get popped for that shit. Foot patrol was dandy dig. It gave me the fresh air I needed to pontificate my plight. I need to get away from this cat Poot he has been bad news since I hook up with him.

Lie after lie and predicament after situation. It's like Kay told me make my mind up or someone will make it for me. I fall subject to any and everything he feels like getting into and now I'm a fkn accessory to a murder. I didn't even know he was going do that shit and here we go though so fk what da fk am I to do. I need to get the fk away from this mtfka soon. I got time as long as he's locked up and put the fk away. I'll get to the house call Kay and run it by her. I noticed the screen was off the side window to the apartment. I keep a screwdriver by the front door just for said occasions. I yelled in the apartment,

"Who's in there?'

"it's me homie wassup?

"don't trip."

"how the fk you get in my shit?"

"better yet how you beat me here?"

"Site and release on the warrants."

"They couldn't hold me for shit I know my rights I been locked up enough shit!"

"What they say to you?"

"nothing real the big the usual shit."

"you didn't tell them shit did you?"

"about what?"

"Good shit I hope that is how you were with them."

"Wow,"

" I heard the fk outta that playboi"

" you got me fkd up."

"nga if I thought that we would not be talking about it you can bet that n your next breathe."

"I don't doubt that."

I seen Poot shoot a couple mtfkz before so to hear him say that I never though twice as to weather or not he was serious the fact that he said it was enough. I viewed it as a Freudian slip a thought buried in his mind that has been festering to surface and I was not about to challenge him, Fuck! Fk! I'm thinking to myself I cain't get away from Poot for shit and this mtfks beat me me back, how?'

"look I'm hell tired I'm a fallout in the room I'll get at you in the morning"

"cool"

"you need a nightlight?

"Fuuuu Quuue!"

I made my way to my bedroom finally I get some piece of mind and time to think this shit out. Smelling the room made me think of Kay immediately and looking aroung not seeing her made me sad. What does Capone think I'msure he misses his dad but ican't get them no further involved with this fool and his dumb shit. What the fk am I going to do about this murder shit I need holla at my dude and see what he think. What I need to do is shake this cat for a minute he on me tuff cause he think I'm a snitch on him nut I ain't that ain't my way. After talking to my Uncle Boomie he helped me come to the best conclusion because Lemm is wild out Commando

"you gadda ice dat cat dawg, I'll help."

If that was coming from anybody else I'd question it but that nga nutty enough but I want mine to live for me not die and kill. Dave had his way but it was complicated and took too much time. Uncle had the right idea I needed to get this nga to cop to the body in order to be cleared. Which is going to be difficult when I can not even figure out how he got to my house before me? I tried over and over but still no contact with Kay I'm starting to worry. This is the longest we been apart since we were married a year ago June 1st, 1995 2 pm.. It was hard for me to sleep so I was up all night thinking, wondering, and worrying. I needed answers and nobody was being straight with me. I'm under 24 hour surveillance my every move is being observed by this lunatic. I finally nodded off about three in the morning only to be awaken 3 hours later by Poot on his phone discussing with someone about the Bone situation.

"Everything went according to plan on my end and what about you?"

"did he bite?"

"no it was right in front of him and he didn't say anything to you huh."

"I knew he was solid which is good or him."

"you tell Travis he almost broke my fkn neck tripping me like that."

"back to the bidness though I took car of bone he wont be molesting anymore lil boys for show and I made him feel every motion."

"you can assure the bosses it's a done deal and thank you for not touching my dude I knew he was solid."

"but I understand the "Conglomerate" has it's rules and regulations believe me I respect it."

"I live it and I would die tryna kill a mtfka attempting to disrespect the cause."

"so I'll be in touch me and folks got a lil celebrating to do I gadda break the good news to him he passed orientation."

"I will wait to hear from you before moving on to the next phase."

"until them family."

"one"

This shit is starting to make more sense but fk this nga is on some way far out. I mean he planned to kill Bone from the gate then that was a fkn hit. He used me to make it happen but he didn't kill me? Then he said he almost broke his neck when he was tripped but it seemed like he knew the guy on the phone? He was

all buddy buddy with them that had to be the officer from the restaurant but what? He has told me way too many lies and it not adding the fk up. I now I find out a accessory to a hit and it was all premeditated. Poot also said that Bone molested somebody I know in my heart if a mtfka put a hand on Capone he might as well dig a fkn grave because there ain't no coming back from that shit fk that no way no how. Murder was the case that they'd give me! I gadda keep this shit on the low or he gone know I know because I don't known when he was planning on telling me wassup. But I did hear him say thank you for not killing my fam could he mean me? That is why I say this shit is not spreading to smooth if you can catch my drift. I still ain't figured how the fk this mtfka beat me to the house he say he got sighted and released but how he get here before me? I didn't see him pass or was I just that fkn out of it on my way home? I gadda use the fkn bathroom plus I remember it is still some left over spaghetti from when Kay cooked last Wednesday. I need to just confront this kat head up like and quit bullshitting cause I need to know what da fk is going on.

Chapter 9 – Assimilation

Processing the information

*J*ust when I thought Poot didn't know what da fk he was

going to do next I find myself having to get answers from him. If he killed Bone on a hit because he molested a lil boy, then who's lil boy and who's running this shit? Where does the trail end? Why did the fkn police fk with me? How long have they really been following Poot and why they ain't busted his ass yet? This shit was driving me bananas and the pressure on my bladder was building. I had to go now so I crept out the room hoping to not disturb this fool asleep on the couch I would continue my investigation in the morning. I went to the bathroom quietly and got me some spaghetti from the kitchen and returned to my room. Watched a Crime SCI episode and fell asleep. I awoke on

Saturday morning rested because for the first time in a few night I knew what I was going to do the nest day and I was going to talk to Poot and get to the bottom of his mess. I woke up in the morning and Poot was nowhere in sight.

No note or nothing the mtfka just vanished at least he was courteous enough to fold his blankets and clean the dishes in the sink left from us being in and out the last couple days. I was wondering where the fk this cat up and bounced to I felt abandoned. It was weird for a minute I come to expect his presents and when he wasn't here when

I expected it threw me off for a minute.

(Wow I'm a codependent ha ha haa sympathizing with my capture.) Then it hit me I could be getting my shit together making the necessary preparation so I can run my sting "operation mockingbird" that is the code name we came up with for the sting on Poot. I had been getting bits and pieces of my plan to Lem, Dave, and my Uncle Roy but I had not had he opportunity to chop it thick. I hit lem

"wassup bra bra"

"wattitdoo my nig?"

"I been waiting to get a hold of you mayne I been tryna get that message to Kay but no response homie."

"I thought she got the first one I left on the answering machine but I was at Cut house yesterday and Tracy came though."

"she said she ain't seen Kay in a few days."

"damb!."

"I knew this nga was up to something."

"what you mean?"

"I think this nga Poot got my Boo and seed pimp."

"he gone like that?"

"I don't know what da fk is going on but I know he been on me like a tattoo for a couple days since that shit popped off and now all of a sudden I can't find this nga in the daytime with a flashlight."

"he's got me into a bunch of shit and I don't know what the fk to do and now I found out that was a hit on Bone."

"This nga is affiliated with some

"conglomerate" or some shit they was talking bout plus this mtfka gets arrested and beat me back to my house!"

"you know what you gadda do right?"

"no, I really don't."

"you gadda change the rules in your favor make him play your game."

"you absolutely right goodlookin I'm holla, one."

What Lem was saying made a lot of damb since I need to stop thinking what he might do from my point of view but more like what I would do if I was in his shoes. I don't have all the fact though so I need to gather more information on him like he did me. Poot watched me for a while and studied my movements and for what? Why do I peak his interest so much we really weren't that tight growing up but we associated with the same kind of people. I 'm going back to square one the corner store there is where Poot and I had our first encounter why did he pick that day? He also told me

"I didn't pick you I chose you."

I hope Kay and Capone are alright where ever they are I can't stop thinking about them. If I find out they are harmed in anyway I'll have a meltdown but If I discover Poot is behind it I'm going to the pen. I hopped in the shower and cleaned myself up in preparation for my day of finding out what the fk Poot has been up to for the last couple years. I hit the pool hall where all the street hustlers go to wind down after a day on the hard grind. I was dead though there was a few new booties in there but nobody I recognized. Jimmy the bartender wasn't even there I guess I came in a lil early there was a youngster there that said no alcohol before 2pm. After that I made my way to the park and tried to see if there was anybody there that could give me some info on this cat but no. I went by the community center to see if anyone was talking bout the murder or seen Poot but no luck. Ain't nobody heard or seen a damb thang they say no news is good news. How did the officers hear about the so called hit but ain't nobody on the street talking? That got me to thinking shit just might be ok on that end and they was fishing for a response.

The police really didn't know shit that is why they gaffled Poot and let him go and they had nothing on me so they had to let me be. I was on my way back to the house even though that shit was panning out I still ain't heard from my girl and I'm really starting to worry and create horrible scenarios because I don't have all the answers. Maybe she fkn somebody else no my girl loves me like I love her. Did she figure out what the fk the deal is or is she hot thinking I'm fkn somebody else. Fk I can't deal with this shit too much longer I need to get at her soon. Made it to the crib and I' going to relax for the time being but to my surprise again this mtfka is at the shack waiting outside.

"wassup playboi?"

"Lounging, I went looking for you."

"you found me now what?"

"I got and you was gone so I kinda panic'd."

"ain't that sweet you and queering up on me is you?"

"Just playing fam."

"truth be told I had few lose ends to tie up and I went to the store to get us some breakfast."

"show my appreciation to my host."

"thanks but I ain't in the mood much for eating I miss Kay and Capone and I ain't heard from them in a minute I'm hella worried."

"I been meaning to talk to you about that."

"huh?"

"about what my family, what the fk did you do to my family nga?"

"slow down pimp, first of all hey are ok."

"you mean to tell me you know where the fk they are?"

"the bosses wanted an insurance policy I told them it would not be necessary but they insisted and without my knowledge it was handled I only found out at the restaurant.

"What the fk you got my family in?"

Chapter 10 – Empathy

Getting sponsored

 "I need you to trust me and ain't shit gone happen to your family"

 "where the fk are they and what is going on?"

 "Okay here we go, I have been watching you for a year or so now."

 "this is the way we recruit."

"I had to know that I could trust you under any circumstances so I created a few of my own."

"so the police was right?"

"ow yea that was no police either."

"I kinda figured that but what is this shit all about?"

"Bone was a hit."

"He molested one of the bosses nephews unaware of who he was fkn with."

"a real sick son of a bitch that destroyed a child's innocence so he had to pay."

"I had a green light from the day I stepped out the pen."

"I have previous engagements, obligations to a purpose higher then myself."

"I'm just following orders."

"you should be celebrating you passed orientation."

"you are on you way to be coming part of the "conglomerate"

"how does it feel lil brother?

"orientation?"

"what the fk are you talking about dood?"

"everything you have been through was all about orientation."

"the conglomerate has to be able to implicitly trust the family members."

"look."

" Bone was a hit, I didn't get arrested at the restaurant those were family members."

"The two officers you met Wells and Vargas those are my sponsors."

"I did that to see if you were going to snitch on me about the Bone situation."

"You family Kay and Capone are safe."

"I must applaud you on your effort to keep them out the picture but it was too late I told you that in the car on the way to your house that night."

"I also got newspapers from the last three days and there is no mention of the situation in the paper so I know you ain't told nobody shit."

"the bosses didn't know you like I do so they took out and insurance policy."

"after I tried to catch you up the first time you kinda lost it so I had to come up with another way to assure you went along with my plan I had to improvise accordingly."

"like you when you came up with the plan to dump the car and body shit like that I essential to running a business."

"those are skills you can't put on no application."

"I respect you and how smart you are on some real shit."

"that is how you got here I was speaking on you to my sponsors and they wanted you to meet the one above me."

"plus they wanted to see for themselves how you would react to a lil pressure and personal turmoil."

"like in the army when the do psychological evaluations and training camps all different forms of brainwashing through a series of commands rigorist exercises; individual mental deprivation."

"accept we are not trying to make you into something you are not we need you to be who you are at your best along side us as a family."

"when I first went to the pen I had no direction, no guidance, and no will to gain any. For whatever purpose that is where my journey for self-respect came in to play. It was only when I was stripped of my material possessions did I begin to look at the me that was me."

"I ain't saying I was happy to be in jail but it leveled out the playing field for ngs like me and it felt good to belong even if it was behind bars incarcerated, and caged away from society."

"we begin to build a new life different from watching what seems like everyone living and enjoying life but you and your kind."

"I hated going to school hungry every morning and on the days I could stomach the walk after puking up bile from being so starved. I couldn't focus cause I had to get money, get wass coming to me."

"that use to be my motivating factor and ended me up In a gang of shit that I did not want to fall subject to."

"I have been educating myself my whole life and I ain't made the right decisions all the time or mark he correct bubbles on they tests but I been surviving on my own and I'm still here."

"I said all that to say this I found my place and I know what I want to do with my life."

"The conglomerate has giving me focus."

"when they heard how well I speak of you it interested them how I could be so uniquely fit and I look up to another mans intelligence."

"they had to meet you."

"when do I get to see Kay and Capone?"

"soon my brother, soon."

"I'm waiting to hear the next phase myself, honestly."

"But do you have any other questions about wass going on?"

"I mean have I caught you up to speed do you feel better?"

"I miss my son Capone and my boo Kay."

"I can't stop thinking about them."

"believe me they are alright you are

"doing what you need to do in making sure that relax, lets go have a good time."

"forgetabbout it tonight we celebrate, huh, your orientated!"

"I want to but I got a lot on my mind"

Damb this is some crazy shit this nga really broke it down to me and the funny thing is I really believe what he is saying but how do I know I can trust who he trust just cause he trust them. I'm not sure he has such a keen sense on his judge of character, but I did say before he seemed older more mature. Wise enough to get me involved in this shit and smart enough to make it so I can't walk the fk away. That in it self alarms me how he has been so manipulative. I mean they got my family and now they want me to be a member what if I say no?

Then they will kill Capone and Kay for sure. I miss them so bad and I'll do what ever the fk I have to getting them back. I wish I was at the store right now sweeping up the floor or restocking the shelves you don't miss that kinda shit until it's gone. I'm caught the fk up for sure. I ain't seen Kay or Capone in a week at least and I don't even know for certain if I will ever see them alive again.

This mtfka gave me exactly what I asked for like the fkn devil in disguise. I didn't know that tryna cut corners and get a lil extra cash to feed my family would be the reason I don't get to be with and enjoy my family, fk!. Look what I got myself into not listening to my boo and she was right the whole fkn time. I didn't understand what I was saying when I was telling Poot I wanted to come up. I want my family alive so I will play my part until I can find my escape route. I don't know if I want to trust Poot even now but I do have to depend on him for now.

Chapter 11 – Responsibility?

Obligated acceptance

Weather or not I chose to be apart of what going now I'm

affiliated and will be convicted by association regardless so I'm

riding this shit. I made my mind up to do what is necessary to

ensure my families safety so I'm participating fully. I passed

Orientation and it was time to celebrate so Poot said we were

going to Reno to kick back and let a lil tie pass before we go to work. I was not really sure what back to work meant but I was starting to enjoy the fact that I was living a lil bit but in the back of my mind I kept thinking about Kay and Capone every time I'd bring it up Poot would tell me that in due time things would be straight but the bosses want to make sue I'm making y adjustment s and transitions. From what I understand in order to become family you have to lose contact with the outside world it's like a sub-society beneath the everyday life regular people live. That is why we often refer to the as civilians unaware of what goes on around them. If people really knew how much junk, toasters, whitegurl, bobby brown, trees, and syrup is sold in they face every day it would scandalize America. I mean at shopping mall parking lots, liquor stores, restaurants, and coffee shops transactions are taking place in plain site that is the world we live in the GAME is deep. Next thing is to clear your name so they run a credit check and get you cleaned up on every smidgen you owe so no red flags go up if you name was ever to get ran. The man is separated from the family so there is focus and it helps you gain trust for the fact they got your family in case you ever get locked up. That is not a factor being everything is ran so smooth we got politicians, local police, DEA, ATF, FBI, task, and Guardian Angels on payroll; hell even a couple ex-military cats from Desert Storm. If they are not getting paid then they work under someone who is getting paid. It is a system set up to insure the machine runs smooth as a can grease. I don't know as much as I would like know but I am getting there and I seem to be working my way up.

Marcos (the waiter)

I found out the guy I thought was a waiter Marcos owned the restaurant and he has been a committed member over 20 years. I have been chasing money my whole life and these guys swim in it and I want that for me and mines maybe it was not such a bad idea to get involved with Poot after all accept for not being able to see Kay and Capone I'm straight. I have been stacking me up some bread fkn with this nga too so I will be able to do a lot more for them it feels good knowing that. I spent a whole year working that fkn job to get nothing and I can't see myself ever coming up from that position and what am I showing my son Capone that you should work even if it don't get you nowhere. It don't seem to be happiness for me and my family ion that design sop I'm a makes a few changes to the blueprint and venture out to see how far this shit goes because lord knows I been hustling hard n the paint to get the gudda. I tried doing the rap thang but every nga can't be 2PAC. I was fkn around in the real-estate market but they wanted a slave for free until I got a license to fk people that don't trust me anyway. I couldn't fk with that wearing a suit shit everyday smiling and I was broke fk dat I need immediate gratification that is why I was grinding and jacking in the first fkn place. If not for Capone and Kay I would have been dead or in jail a long time ago. My life left in my hands ain't amounting to shit. I'm like the devil's advocate his personal workshop without a purpose that is why I gadda get them back. Going along wit this ngs shit will help me achieve that goal. Long as I stay in control of myself I should be okay and stay on my toes. I have come to terms with the fact I can't see my family now I must get to work getting them back. I still need to know more about this "conglomerate" who else is involved and how many members? Where they are keeping my family? How long does this shit take to process and what the fk they expected of me? Poot's attitude toward me has changed a lot since he received the news I passed my orientation he was more easy going everything wasn't so serious and now I'm the one on point and poised. I have to study him now because I always feel like he knows something I don't. I need to see how he communicates with the bosses and how he receives his orders. When we went out we went to the same restaurant that he was supposedly arrested at. Low and behold the same two guys that were supposed to be police were sitting there at a table with the guy that tackled Poot and the waiter except they were all in suits now but there was no one else in the restaurant. Poot walked me passed the table to the table in back again. He left the room and I could see him greeting them. They had a brief exchange of words and then one of the gentle man made a gesture, and a waiter came out the back handed Poot an envelope he put it in the front pocket of his leather jacket turned around came back to the table. We had a drink and left the restaurant again. When we got to the car Poot turned to me and opened his jacket for the envelope opened it took out twenty-five hundred dollars and gave it to me.

"I am responsible for you under conglomerate law I brought you in."

"I had to accept that or you would have   had to go when I killed Bone."

"we are brothers if you steal from me you are stealing from yourself if you lie to me you are lying to me you are lying to yourself."

"I only tell you this because from here on out it ain't no joke we are bound by obligation."

"You want to see you family and I want you to se you family but there is one thing the bosses ask of you before it can be so and you will be free to see you family."

"not only that but you will not want for anything else after."

"you are conglomerate we need nothing and no one, self contained."

"anything you ask of me I will do."

"the conglomerated has my loyalty and dedication."

"you will not regret this decision."

"Today is the first day of you new life, a rebirth so to speak."

Chapter 12 – Indentured Servitude

A state of mind.

So now I have a new life with the world at my fingertips. It

is a bit unsettling not knowing where Capone and Kay are and if they are even to together. I really don't like this but I must make the best of it. I will see them again one day soon. When we reunite it will all have been worth it. I have to focus for now and keep myself alive. Learn all I can and make the right moves to gain my position. I gadda watch this mtfka real close cause regardless there is a lot to be learned from this nga Poot. I am dedicated to my word and if what they say is right then I will remain loyal. I have been searching all my life for that feeling of belonging and now I might have found it. I want to see my family and be assured of they safety and then I will be convinced. So it looks like I'm going along for the ride.

"I'd like to propose a toast."

"To the Omega Conglomerate!"

"and it's eternal success!"

there was a thunderous roar! Here Here!

THE END

To be continued................

266 Greendale Way - Suite 3

San Jose, CA. 95129

(408) 561-5297

www.myspace.com/organizedcriminalz

www.myspace.com/ahitchy

mstrkna@yahoo.com

USBN   978-0-615-20495-6

This book has been dedicated to my brother Andre Wells.
To anybody who has beeen through or down with turning struggle into hustle Thank you.

Thank you to my mother Terri L Wells and Khyree Branch, Tina Meehlieb for accepting my busy schedule.

Thank you to all my supporters, fans, and family.

ORGANIZED 4 LIFE !!!!!!!!!!!!!

NO MO ENTERPRISE
STATE of the ARC

COMING SOON

www.myspace.com/ahitchy

www.myspace.com/organizedcriminalz

buy the muzik support the independent

only available on line,,,

Catch yo boi lemm pill popppin again...

Thizz time he's got hiz own batch

www.myspace.com/lemmonyvonblew

MOMO ENTERPRISE PRESENTS:

QUADRANT POLOTIX

HOW THE FOUR CONERS OF THE BAY COLABORATE, CAMPAINE, AND POLOTIC.

Slappin mixtape with a few hot family appearances

Only available online

www,cdbaby.com/organizedcrim

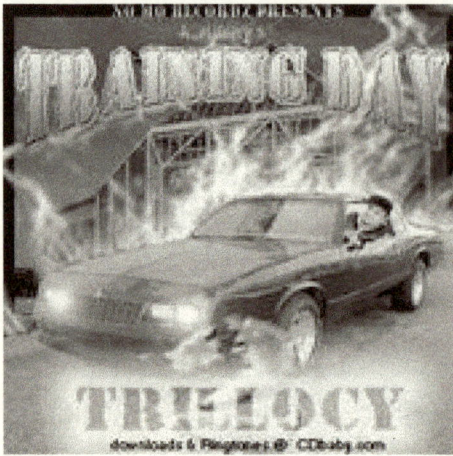

Coming sooon

Only available online

www,cdbaby.com/organizedcrim

Only available online

www,cdbaby.com/organizedcrim

Only available online

www,cdbaby.com/organizedcrim

V da pimp

Tearin a chunk out the game as the

Coming

soon

Coming soon

Nomo Enterprise not just a group of rappers but a family of entertainers, founded in 1992 by Draden Branch gka Hitchler Rose.

Has now grew into a multifaceted conglomerate of businessmen dedicated to the sole purpose of helping each

other progress

Independently.

It ain't the same without you Sav so until you get out we riding for you.

www.ingramcontent.com/pod-product-compliance
Lightning Source LLC
Chambersburg PA
CBHW031845090426
42741CB00005B/363